D1124178

DENIS LEARY'S
MERRY F***IN' CHRISTMAS

By Denis Leary and Chris Phillips

Illustrated by Corky Quakenbush

COMEDY CENTRAL BOOKS

RUNNING PRESS
PHILADELPHIA · LONDON

Books published by Running Press are available at special discounts for bulk
purchases in the United States by corporations, institutions, and other organizations.
For more information, please contact the Special Markets Department at the
Perseus Books Group, 2300 Chestnut Street, Suite 200, Philadelphia, PA 19103, or
call (800) 810-4145, ext. 5000, or e-mail special.markets@perseusbooks.com.

ISBN 978-0-7624-4762-6

E-book ISBN 978-0-7624-4771-8

9   8   7   6   5   4   3   2   1
Digit on the right indicates the number of this printing

Design: Joshua McDonnell
Editor: Greg Jones
Typography: Duality

Running Press Book Publishers
2300 Chestnut Street
Philadelphia, PA 19103-4371

Visit us on the web!
www.runningpress.com
www.comedycentral.com
www.denisleary.com

The authors would like to thank Jesus, bourbon, tinsel, Hermie the Dentist, dysfunctional families and NyQuil. Especially NyQuil.

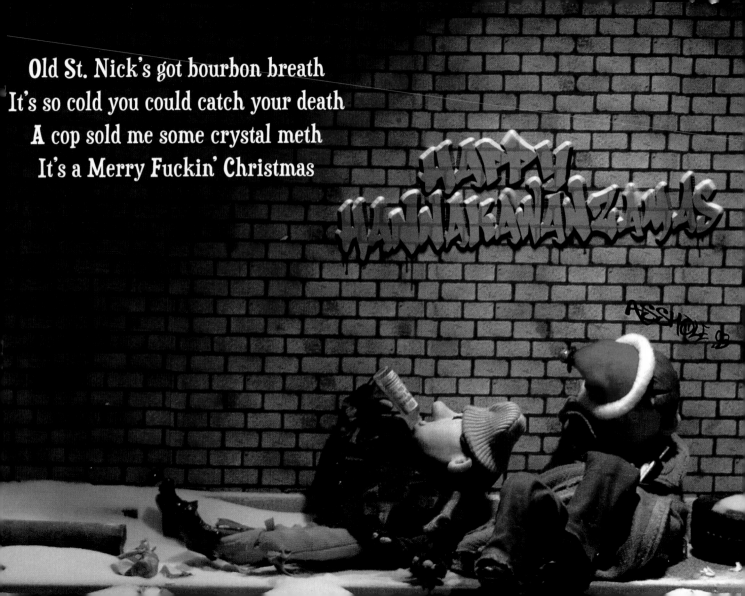

Old St. Nick's got bourbon breath
It's so cold you could catch your death
A cop sold me some crystal meth
It's a Merry Fuckin' Christmas

HAPPY HANNUKKAWANZZAWMAS

ASSHOLE

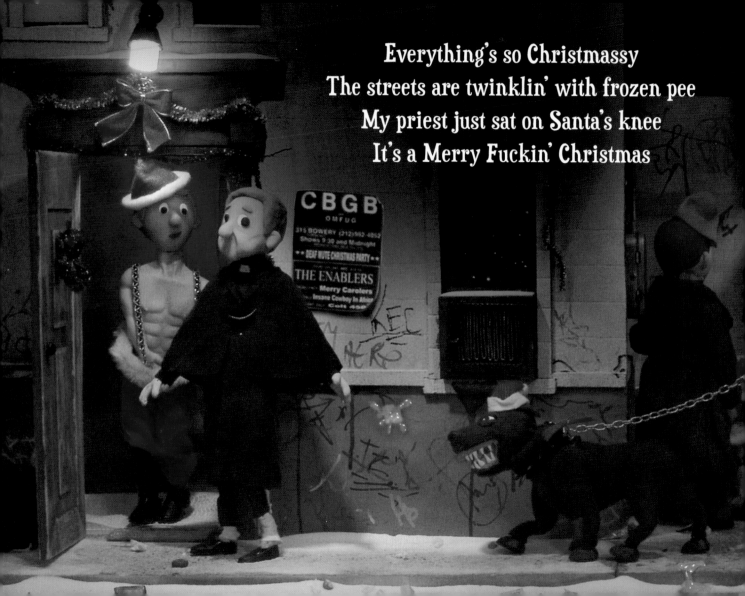

Everything's so Christmassy
The streets are twinklin' with frozen pee
My priest just sat on Santa's knee
It's a Merry Fuckin' Christmas

All the kids go to bed each night
To dream what Santa brings 'em . . .

. . . Unless they're Jewish or Muslim
Or some other gyp religion.

Blinding lights hung on every block
Icy fingers and frozen snot
My snowman's got a carrot cock
It's a Merry Fuckin' Christmas

People giving to charities

And dropping cash in buckets . .

Relatives we love to hate
Show up early and stay too late
I'd rather lick a reindeer's taint
It's a Merry Fuckin' Christmas

Santa's just some nice old guy
Who waits for this all summer . . .

Cracklin' fires to keep me warm
And my collection of Asian porn
Cradle my bells and work my horn . . .

It's a keep on truckin' Last year suckin' Midget chuckin' Slap the puck in

How much wood could a woodchuck chuck in
Merry Fuckin' Christmas!